TAURUS

James Petulengro

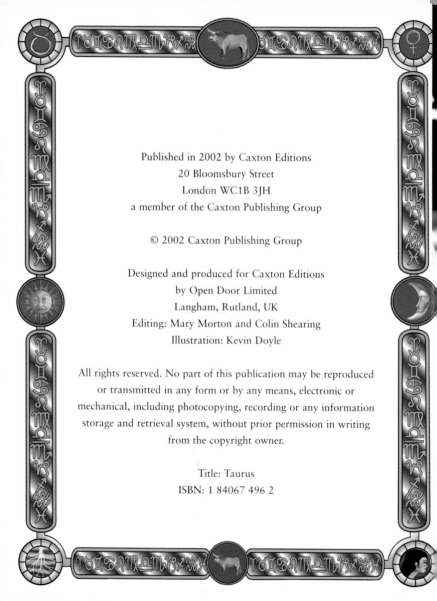

Published in 2002 by Caxton Editions
20 Bloomsbury Street
London WC1B 3JH
a member of the Caxton Publishing Group

© 2002 Caxton Publishing Group

Designed and produced for Caxton Editions
by Open Door Limited
Langham, Rutland, UK
Editing: Mary Morton and Colin Shearing
Illustration: Kevin Doyle

Title: Taurus
ISBN: 1 84067 496 2

TAURUS
CONTENTS

TAURUS
INTRODUCTION

The art and science of astrology has been around for over 5,000 years and is still used by many people for many different purposes. The scientific aspect of the subject is in the astronomical calculations required to make a birth chart. A birth chart (horoscope) is like a photographic image of the planets in the sky above you when you are born. No two people in the world have the same birth chart; it is totally unique to you and is what defines your individuality. You may have many things in common with other people, but the complete birth chart is yours and yours alone. The artistic aspect of the subject is in the interpretation of the position of these planetary bodies. In this book we shall be looking particularly at the positions of the Sun and the Moon at the time of your birth and how these affect your life.

Introduction

You may find that if you were born from the 19th to the 23rd of the month your Sun sign is what is called "on the cusp". Each year the Sun enters the various Sun signs on different days so just because you were born on the 21st of the month, for example, does not necessarily mean you are the Sun sign you think you are. Calculating your birth chart will help you to discover exactly what your Sun sign is.

As a special feature, if you do not have one already, you can calculate your own birth chart including a short 8-page interpretation on my website at http://www.jamespetulengro.co.uk type in your birth details and you can then print out astrological details and your birth chart. This may also help you when you come to look at the Moon sign part of this book and the Sun and Moon combinations if you do not know your Moon sign.

Introduction

The 12 Zodiac signs are traditionally formed into four groups within which they interact and complement each other.

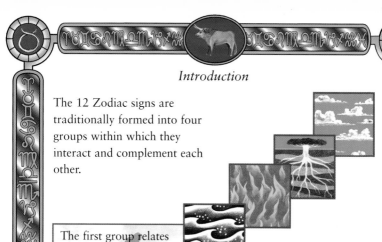

The first group relates to the elements. These consist of fire signs, earth signs, air signs and water signs. The fire signs are by nature enthusiastic and comprise Aries, Leo and Sagittarius. The earth signs are Taurus, Virgo and Capricorn and are practical. The air signs are Gemini, Libra and Aquarius and are intellectual. The water signs are Cancer, Scorpio and Pisces which are emotional.

A second group is known as the qualities. The cardinal signs are Aries, Cancer, Libra and Capricorn who tend to be outgoing. The fixed signs of Taurus, Leo, Scorpio and Aquarius tend to be rigid in their opinions. The mutable signs of Gemini, Virgo, Sagittarius and Pisces are flexible and adaptable.

Introduction

The third group refers to positivity/masculinity and negativity/femininity. The positive signs are Aries, Gemini, Leo, Libra, Sagittarius and Aquarius. These people tend to be extroverts. The negative/feminine signs are Taurus, Cancer, Virgo, Scorpio, Capricorn and Pisces and these signs make people introvert. Do not be confused if you are Taurus man as this does not mean that you lack masculinity any more than a woman with a masculine Sun sign such as Sagittarius lacks femininity.

Lastly the fourth group is known as the polarities. This indicates the special relationship a sign has with its polar opposite. Polar signs complement each other so that there is a special rapport and understanding between them. For example, as Taurus is the most stable of signs, Scorpio, its polar opposite, is the Zodiac sign of people with a powerful need to change. Ruling planets – each sign is ruled by one of the planets, and each planet has a very similar energy to the sign it rules. For example Taurus is ruled by Venus, the goddess of beauty.

SUN SIGNS

WHAT ARE THEY?

The Sun is the star at the centre of our solar system which is composed of nine planets. The Earth is the third one out, at a distance of 93 million miles. The Sun is 109 times the size of the Earth and without it there would be no life. It is the most powerful of all the bodies in our solar system and exerts a gravitational pull upon all of us. It affects each of our personalities so strongly that a person who is born under a particular sign will continue to have those characteristics throughout their life. The Sun is the fuel of our solar system, just as the Sun is the fuel of your personality.

Your Sun sign or sign of the Zodiac depends on the month of the year that you were born in because the Earth travels around the Sun once in approximately 365 days and the Sun appears to travel through one of 12 constellations in the sky above.

Sun Signs – What are They?

Looking at your Sun sign should not be confused with studying the daily horoscopes that you will find in magazines or newspapers. In this book we are examining the effect that your Sun sign has on your personality rather than predictions. You were born between 21st April and 21st May which makes you a Taurus.

Some astrologers feel that the Sun sign readings are too much of a generalisation, as if all butchers, bakers and candlestick makers were the same. However, the Sun, as I said earlier, is the most powerful body in our whole life which is reflected in the accuracy of Sun sign readings.

If you know someone's Sun sign you are most certainly much more informed about that person than not knowing it.

Your Sun sign personality is the personality that you present to people because it is what you cherish and is what you are most proud of about yourself. To be more specific the placement of your Sun represents how you express your ego. In general a person's Sun sign will represent how they present themselves to the world during daylight hours and their Moon sign will represent how they present themselves as dusk arrives and their more intimate, hidden side comes out.

MOON SIGNS
WHAT ARE THEY?

The Moon is the Earth's satellite and is approximately 250,000 miles away. Although only small in diameter, 2,160 miles, the Moon exerts considerable gravitational influence on the Earth and is responsible for the tides. It orbits the Earth in approximately 28 days, known as the lunar cycle, and passes through each sign of the Zodiac every 2.5 days. In your birth chart it is considered almost as important as the Sun, but its influences are different. The Moon holds sway over your moods and emotional life. Whereas the Sun is your day, the Moon represents your night.

Your Moon sign represents how you deal with and express your tender, caring side and your emotional responses in general. It represents your instinctive, unconscious, primitive, habitual personality. How you express yourself is affected by your Moon sign. It represents

Moon Signs – What are They?

your basic emotional needs and how you interact with others. It represents your gut instinct and how you react to things when you are caught by surprise, particularly when you feel you are threatened. Another important area that the Moon controls is that of your domestic arena. Since it is the planet that rules Cancer the Moon is seen as feminine, watery, negative and reflective.

Some people do have the same sign for the Sun and the Moon, so both their ego and emotions are ruled by the same sign. This will generally provide a pattern of consistency through many situations in your life.

Above: the Moon is seen as feminine, watery, negative and reflective.

TAURUS
THE SUN SIGN

If you are a Taurus and if we met and I began to explain to you your personality through your horoscope, the most I would get out of you would be a "uh-uh". Taurus is the strong, silent type.

Taurus

21st April to 21st May

Positive Traits

Reliable, sturdy, strong, patient, warm-hearted, loving, placid

Negative Traits

Possessive, greedy, jealous, envious, resentful, self-indulgent, stubborn

Traditional Associations

Zodiac Symbol: The Bull
Glyph: ♉
Ruling Planet: Venus
Ruling House: The Second
Gender: Feminine and Negative
Polarity: Scorpio
Element: Earth
Quality: Fixed
Key Phrase: I Own
Body Area: The Throat and Neck
Colour: Brown or blue
Metal: Copper
Gemstone: Emerald Lapis Lazuli
Foods: Cereals, apples, pears, vines, artichokes, clove, sorrel
Flora: Rose, daisy, violet, poppy, vine, apple, ash, fig, pear, crab apple
Countries: Cyprus, Iran, Switzerland, Ireland
Cities: Lucerne, Palermo, Parma, Dublin
Tarot Card: The Hierophant
Deities: Venus and Aphrodite
Activity: Singing

Taurus – the Sun Sign

Taurus is an earth sign and is ruled by the planet Venus, the goddess of beauty. As a fixed sign they are inflexible in their opinions and find it hard to accept change.

This is a feminine sign, whether you are a man or a woman, even though it is symbolised by a Bull, a male creature. This may seem a strange contradiction but that is the essence of Taurus.

As the second sign of the Zodiac, Taurus represents stability. The Bull is happiest in its own field, grazing away at life. A typical Taurus will move deliberately and speak sparingly and, once their mind is made up, they will seldom change it for any reason. Usually they just want to be left alone. Don't disturb them and they remain content; press them and they become obstinate. Shove too hard or tease too much and they will explode.

They may go on for months on end showing perfect poise and control, then, quite unexpectedly, someone will push them a little too far and they will snort, begin to paw the earth, narrow their eyes and charge at full speed. The best advice is to get out of the way as fast as possible.

A Bull won't be moved unless the grass in the next field is much greener.

Taurus – the Sun Sign

Taurus people are calm and seldom lose their temper. When they do, they put their heads down and can destroy anything in their path. Ask any matador! Some Bulls have such control that they may not even charge more than once or twice in their whole life but when they do it is demolition derby time.

Taureans are also about as stubborn as humans can be. Once a Bull has made up their mind nothing can move them. Many Bulls can put up with physical and emotional burdens for years in silence without complaint. Their loyalty and devotion to family and friends often surpass understanding. Many Taurus people deserve gold medals

for courage in bearing the blows of fate that would long ago have broken other Sun signs.

Bulls do not understand subtle humour but show them a slapstick comedy and they will fall about. Their humour is warm and earthy, reminiscent of William Shakespeare's (himself a Taurus) Falstaff. They are seldom cruel or vindictive, but a Bull and their possessions are rarely parted and they can sometimes seem mean because of this. Taureans like to build their empires slowly and surely. They like to accumulate power along with their wealth, but this is mainly for the sheer enjoyment of possessing it. Just knowing

Taurus – the Sun Sign

that they have power along with money satisfies the Bull's sense of security. Also it is particularly important to Bulls that others know what they have and so they will display their possessions to all and sundry, including showing off their lovers.

Above: Bulls will display their possessions to all and sundry, including showing off their lovers.

Taurus – the Sun Sign

Taurus people are impressed by size – the bigger, the better. As Bulls are ruled by Venus beautiful paintings, classical art and great music stir them deeply. Many of them are also collectors of antiques and every Taurean home will be full of their prized possessions that they love to put on display.

Music is a strong feature in their lives, too. They often have delightful singing voices and many opera singers fall under the sign of Taurus.

The Taurean mind is sensible and shows great clarity and is usually very interested in how they can own more than they have. They love the earthy tones of nature, particularly when they are printed on bank notes. There is nothing small about Taurus, including their capacity for lasting love and their potential for wealth.

Copper, the metal of Taurus, is an excellent conductor and its burnished beauty glows for years.

Venus showers them with luxury throughout their lives and their homes are beautiful places. The sensual Bull loves to bathe in perfumed water, surrounded by candles.

The Bull may be slow and steady but eventually success comes to them. When it does they are well prepared.

Taurus – the Sun Sign

Taurus is as patient as Time and as deep as the Earth. Their dependable strength can and does move mountains. Bulls are more takers than givers and usually see everyone they encounter as potential suppliers. That does not mean to say they are not generous. The Bull will give you their time and their loyalty and their loving affection.

Above: the Bull will give you their time and their loyalty and their loving affection.

Taurus – the Sun Sign

The Bull has more moral and emotional courage than many of the masculine signs of the Zodiac. Their self-control is unsurpassed and they have a gracious tendency to take people as they are without fuss. They take people at face value.

Bulls have common sense and a shrewdness which gives them an ability to comprehend the basics of any subject, but they rarely think or read on a deep level. They enjoy coffee-table books on gardening and beautiful homes. Adventures happen to other people or the characters they read about in romantic novels.

Their perspective is very straightforward. Bulls are grounded in their bodies and know what's good for them – the answer is money.

Above: Bulls are grounded in their bodies and know what's good for them - the answer is money.

Taurus – the Sun Sign

Scents, lotions and sensual indulgences all feature heavily in the Bull's surroundings. Colours send their senses soaring. If you want to impress a Bull then take them to the best restaurant in town, followed by the opera. A Bull's sense of touch is extremely refined. This is the most touchy-feely of all the signs. They enjoy hugs and cuddles and love soft fabrics on their bodies. The Bull is usually the one with the designer clothes. Physical comfort is the Bull's be-all and end-all.

The Bull's imperviousness to pain and emotional stress is almost miraculous. They are as dependable and predictable as an old grandfather clock. There is always room enough and love enough to welcome both strangers and relatives to their warm hearths.

Above: Bulls enjoy hugs and cuddles and love soft fabrics on their bodies.

Taurus – the Sun Sign

YOUR BODY

Taurus people typically have a bovine appearance to them. Male Taureans have the muscular neck with broad shoulders of a Bull whereas female Taureans have big eyes with fluttery eyelashes like that of Ermintrude the cow, but naturally more graceful. Taurus people are very slow and indolent in their movements, because Venus, their ruling planet, gives a sensuousness to their form. They always look as if they are contemplating. If you do see a fast Taurus then they have more than likely just lost their temper so make sure you are not the one on the receiving end.

Their hair is often dark and curly or at least they have a slight wave about the forehead, resembling a Bull's forelock. Owing to their love of luxury and good food Taureans have a tendency to put on weight but, as they are usually large-boned people, they carry it well. Indeed Taureans have a definite physical presence. Taurus is an earth sign and Bulls certainly have their feet firmly fixed on the ground.

Above: male Taureans have the muscular neck with broad shoulders of a Bull.

Taurus – the Sun Sign

YOUR POSSESSIONS

Taurus is the most possessive of all the signs of the Zodiac. Their whole being is measured by what they own. They love luxurious surroundings which cost money so they have a tendency to be hard working. The Bull and their money is seldom parted. Not every Taurus is rich, but they certainly have enough to live comfortably. They like to build their empires slowly and steadily. They start small but soon accumulate sound investments with which they can increase their power base and thus fulfil their Venusian desire for sensual enjoyment.

Above: Taurus is the most possessive of all the signs of the Zodiac. Their whole being is measured by what they own.

Taurus – the Sun Sign

HOW YOU COMMUNICATE

Since Taurus rules the throat and neck their speaking voices generally have a lovely resonance and quality to it. Placid-natured on the whole, they tend to speak slowly and assertively. They avoid arguments, simply because they are stubborn enough to believe they are right so do not see the point. They are sparing in their use of language and are more likely to communicate with their bodies when angered. A huffing of the shoulders is a typical reaction of an annoyed Bull. However, beware the full bellowing of an enraged Taurus. They are solid, practical thinkers, with no frills or showy mental gymnastics.

Above: beware the full bellowing of an enraged Taurus. They are solid, practical thinkers, with no frills or showy mental gymnastics.

Taurus – the Sun Sign

YOUR HOME LIFE

Taureans love their domestic environment. They love to laze about in their homes which are comfortable and luxurious. Creature comforts are what they desire most. If they do not own their own home then they are dreaming about it, or reading home and garden magazines and books on interior design. They love being close to the earth and their love of the countryside will come out in one way or another. They may even dabble in property investment but only if there are secure prospects. They like stability and prefer to stay in one place and so lavish attention on their homes all the time.

Entertaining of guests, particularly old friends, is done frequently in the Taurus home, but they only like a few people at a time. They tend to avoid crowds.

Above: Taureans love to laze about in their homes which are comfortable and luxurious.

YOUR CREATIVITY

They have an earthy flare for all culinary pursuits, whether actually creating delectable dishes or just in the eating of them. Another interest they have is landscape gardening and many a Bull has a perfect lawn with borders and bedding.

They invest much time in their children, lavishing affection and warmth on them. Patience is a great virtue of the Taurean and they will see their children through almost anything. However, they expect them to respect all material items in the home and will lay down a firm set of rules to be followed. A child who runs wild breaking things will not be tolerated by

a Taurus and will soon have the Bull snorting and firmly handing out discipline, although this will never be done in a cruel way.

Because of their great love of beauty many Bulls make fine musicians and artists and it is likely that they will have either a fine music collection or a number of instruments or painting materials within their homes.

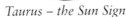

Taurus – the Sun Sign

YOUR HEALTH

The average Bull has a very strong constitution and is usually in good health. It takes a lot to put them on their back and they have stomachs of cast-iron. However, once they are actually ill, it takes them a long time to recuperate, mainly because of their stubborn refusal to obey medical advice. And their natural inclination to pessimism does not help with speedy recovery either.

Since Taurus rules the neck and throat regions one can expect problems with the larynx and the pharynx as well as the thyroid gland. A simple cold often turns into laryngitis. They also encounter problems with their backs and reproductive organs.

Above: once they are actually ill it takes Taureans a long time to recuperate, mainly because of their stubborn refusal to obey medical advice.

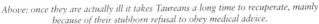

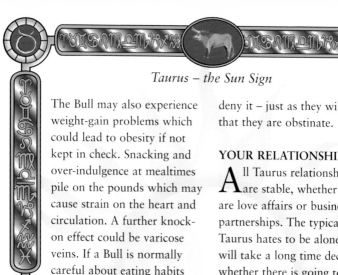

The Bull may also experience weight-gain problems which could lead to obesity if not kept in check. Snacking and over-indulgence at mealtimes pile on the pounds which may cause strain on the heart and circulation. A further knock-on effect could be varicose veins. If a Bull is normally careful about eating habits but still has persistent weight problems then the thyroid gland should be examined as this could be to blame. Gout could also be a problem due to regular intake of excess alcohol.

The main cause of Taurean illness is lack of country air and exercise. Their systems always need both, even though their obstinacy will

deny it – just as they will deny that they are obstinate.

YOUR RELATIONSHIPS

All Taurus relationships are stable, whether they are love affairs or business partnerships. The typical Taurus hates to be alone, but will take a long time deciding whether there is going to be a relationship at all. Taurus has more moral and emotional courage than many of the other signs and once they have made up their mind they stick to their decision.

Bulls are romantic at heart and if they buy gifts they are generous in the extreme. If you get a large, fancy, poetic Valentine, this will undoubtedly be from a Bull

Taurus – the Sun Sign

and when a Taurus courts you, either for business or pleasure, they take their time. They are not wild fantasists and if they tell you their plans for the future then they will have everything carefully worked out. They are highly sentimental and always have favourite songs, favourite colours, favourite foods and favourite places that stay the same throughout their lives.

Above: Bulls are romantic at heart and if they buy gifts they are generous in the extreme.

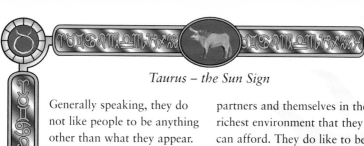

Taurus – the Sun Sign

Generally speaking, they do not like people to be anything other than what they appear. They expect that what they see is what they get. The male Bull finds feminists unsettling as he likes to rule the roost. The female Taurus likes her men to be all male because she is aware of her stubbornness and so needs a strong partner.

Although they have a great deal of self-control in their relationships they do have a deep, physical passion. Bedroom athletics are not their forte, but smouldering, slow sensuality does arouse them. Touch, taste, and perfumes of the luxurious variety all turn them on and they will indulge their

partners and themselves in the richest environment that they can afford. They do like to be out in nature and a roll in the hay is not beyond them.

Once you have embarked on a partnership with a Taurus, you will be treated with gracious consideration. Taurean love is simple, down-to-earth and honest. Loyalty and faithfulness are of the utmost importance to the Bull. Their affection and devotion will ensure that you feel loved. They believe that they own their partners and so will treat them like their most valued possession. However, if their love is not reciprocated they will become moody, withdrawn and will eventually break up the

Taurus – the Sun Sign

relationship in a rage. Never contradict a Taurus in public and do not try to hurry or rush them. They choose their own pace of life and, although they are slow and deliberate, they are not lazy.

If they are accused of such then they feel that their partner is being disloyal and that is unforgivable. Their characteristic pout is a good indication that there are problems ahead.

Above: loyalty and faithfulness are of the utmost importance to the Bull. Their affection and devotion will ensure that you feel loved.

Taurus – the Sun Sign

YOUR RESOURCES

The most important thing for a Taurus is security, particularly financial security. Until they have achieved this, they may appear to be mean and grasping but, once they feel that they are on their way to acquiring their goals, they are generous and will help others to do the same.

Bulls are very good at investment, especially in property, but they do not like speculation because they want to know exactly how much is coming in each week. They prefer set salaries so that their finances can be predicted. They are ambitious but will not take unnecessary risks. These are solid, dependable business people, not flashy sales types. If anyone helps them build their empire then they will share it gladly.

YOUR EDUCATION

When it comes to education Bulls will pursue a practical, vocational subject. They want to learn the things they need to know to establish a secure future for themselves and their family. If they have received a good education then they will take courses specifically to do with their chosen work. Education is only for practical purposes to a Taurus. Knowledge for its own sake is not what they are looking for. Highly educated Bulls, however, will not show it publicly and if anyone attempts to get them into an

Taurus – the Sun Sign

academic conversation they will not find out very much. They keep quiet about their academic achievements and are uninterested in showing off their knowledge.

Above: bulls are solid, dependable business people, not the flashy sales types. If anyone helps them build their empire then they will share it gladly.

YOUR CAREER AND AMBITIONS

A Taurean approaches their career carefully and with great thought. They are looking for something solid that will last them a lifetime; something that will continually bring in a regular income. They have great drive and ambition in whatever they set their minds to do. They are not idealists; they are practical and well grounded in their work.

They make excellent estate agents, bankers, farmers and horticulturists. They can be very happy with a career in the arts, especially when expressing themselves creatively through their senses, but are not prepared to starve to achieve it. There are many Taurean singers and composers, but they are most attracted to the production side of the industry. The one thing they should never be, though, is a salesperson because they are usually sparing with their words.

Once they have decided what their chosen path is going to be, they seldom change their minds and work steadily and quietly on their way to the top. They will soak up knowledge through years of devotion to the job until they are promoted to a high position. They also like routine and sensible hours so that they can enjoy the home that they have so beautifully put together.

Taurus – the Sun Sign

As an employee they tend to be reliable and are quite happy to take orders without resentment. They have a high respect for authority in the knowledge that when they achieve status themselves they will in turn receive that respect.

As an employer they have an inflexible and rigid concept of working methods and, although they will show great patience and aim for perfection, they should not be pushed. The more responsibility they are given, the better they will work. They are dependable, trustworthy and honest.

YOUR FRIENDS

A typical Bull is very careful in their choice of friends. As they are home-loving people, they love to share what they have with their friends. Taureans have a generous heart and will help any friend with a problem. However, they can be deeply possessive and expect their kindness to be reciprocated.

YOUR HOPES AND FEARS

The only hope that the Bull has is that they will acquire beautiful objects, the finances to acquire those objects and a lasting love to share them with. Their greatest fear is, of course, poverty. This will make a Bull physically ill.

THE 12
MOON SIGNS

To find out your moon sign either consult a professional astrologer or go to my website www.jamespetulengro.co.uk for a free birth chart.

ARIES

An Aries Moon means that you are extremely assertive in your nature on a subconscious level. Through the influence of Mars, life to you is one big adventure, with your ego ruling your feelings. You may come across as pushy because of your continual drive for success and your high self-motivation.

You are very open to new ideas and concepts and can make quick decisions based on your instincts. It is rare that you use reasoning skills, preferring instead to leap into action. You often lose your temper over the smallest thing without a thought for the consequences. What you are thinking gets said as your mind is always active and

The 12 Moon Signs

your emotions explode out of you, often before you have thought things through.

You are a bit of a rogue at times, with a "joie de vivre" which attracts many people to you. You are emotionally independent and will develop detachment from the people around you except perhaps from your immediate loved ones whom you will put on a pedestal. You feel with your ego.

Advice is something that you rarely take, preferring instead to rely on your own instincts. If someone gives you advice when it is not asked for you can fly off the handle very quickly. The Moon in Aries can indicate a sense of

insecurity behind your independent and assertive exterior. You love challenges, particularly from a worthy opponent but react emotionally when you lose. You rarely compromise, particularly when it comes to your feelings. However, when it comes to romance someone who can stand up to you will earn your respect.

At home you have an enthusiasm for DIY but you need to be in control of both the design and the work. This can often lead to domestic disputes.

TAURUS

A Taurus Moon means that you place great emphasis on material possessions. Your emotions are focused on getting the best that life has to offer. In terms of comfort, you cannot go without all of life's luxuries. You enjoy making your home environment beautiful and tasteful. You have a great love of collecting things, including people and you can be extremely possessive about your friends and lovers. Emotionally you are very down-to-earth and practical and spend your time working to achieve your material desires in order to lead the good life that you feel you deserve. You have a natural business sense and can be very successful in the world of finance. The Moon is very stable in this sign as your emotional responses are slow but well thought out.

The 12 Moon Signs

As a friend you are good-natured, loyal and easygoing. You rarely lose your temper but, when you do, you can be very formidable. You would rather love than fight and can be very surprised at other people's rages. Small grievances rarely bother you. You have strong physical appetites and a deep emotional need to gratify them. You are very determined but sometimes stubborn and self-indulgent, particularly for the good things in life.

You are a sensual and affectionate lover, and highly sexed, but you have a tendency to be over-possessive as you have a strong sense of ownership with both things and people. Your voice is pleasantly harmonious to others and you may well love singing and dancing and the arts in general as Taurus is ruled by Venus, goddess of beauty.

You are generally very conservative in your outlook and, once you have decided what is true about life, you will stick to it and find change of any kind difficult. You must avoid becoming too narrow-minded in your opinions.

GEMINI

A Gemini Moon makes you witty and articulate with a tendency to feel with your mind. You are adaptable in your ideas and very attracted to mental stimulation. You enjoy socialising and the sign of the twins indicates a happy and easygoing personality. Your trademark is observation and you have a great gift for verbalising all of your ideas. You are friendly and gregarious and will have many friends, lovers and acquaintances. You truly love people of all kinds and being ruled by Mercury, the messenger god, communication is your whole life. You are never at a loss for words but sometimes you can get carried away and end up arguing with yourself, both in your own mind and in conversations and debates. This sometimes confuses people as to what you really believe, as you can change your mind as quickly as you can change your clothes. In fact, you are likely to do both several times during a day.

The 12 Moon Signs

Your moods can be very changeable, up one moment and down the next, and you tend to be nervous in your movements. Some people may think you are shallow, but actually you are torn apart by constantly changing feelings.

Your restless nature is always searching for new stimuli. Although you may not do too well academically you are a life-long student of knowledge itself and, like a butterfly, your mind will flit from subject to subject taking sustenance from each.

You have a great sense of humour and will be very entertaining at parties, although sometimes you can seem too cynical for some people and you can hurt

people with cutting remarks which you will forget as quickly as you said them.

You are romantically inclined but in an intellectual way. You are fascinated more by the mind of your lovers than in their bodies. You are not the most faithful of the signs as you are always looking for something or someone better around the next corner. You are not the domestic type as you are moving around too much to settle down, until perhaps much later in life. You do not like to be tied down to one person or one place; freedom is important to you and you hate being restricted by emotional attachments.

CANCER

A Cancer Moon is highly sensitive due to the fact that it is ruled by the Moon. Therefore, you can be moody and broody and your moods will fluctuate through the month, as the Moon changes from New to Full.

You are highly maternal and will mother all your friends and family if they will let you. You need to be careful not to smother them. You also have a deep and powerful capacity to memorise every experience and to re-experience it in great detail whenever you want. You also have a strong intuition and an almost psychic ability to tune in to other people's thoughts and emotions and to the atmosphere of places. You should trust in your gut feelings and hunches but because you are, by nature, suspicious and distrusting you must be careful that this does not turn into paranoia. Whatever you feel always

remember that the Moon is affecting it. You go through cycles of feeling more than any other sign. You must be careful not to mistake your feelings for the feelings of the people around you that you are picking up on.

You are gentle, peaceful and romantic, and appreciative of all that is feminine in life. You have a great love of home and family which you will protect with your life. Of all the signs you are the greatest homemaker. Your domestic life needs to be safe and secure as this is the shell that the crab that you are will retreat to when disturbed. Some people only see your hard outer shell and forget that inside you are soft and kind.

You are particularly interested in history and your ancestors, and Cancer Moons love their country. You need to feel that you are in control of the whole world and can become withdrawn and ill when you lose control of any part of it. Change is not something that you relish.

Above: you are gentle, peaceful and romantic and appreciative of all that is feminine in life.

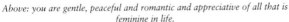

LEO

Leo Moons have a sunny disposition and a desire to lead in all walks of life. You are generally confident, cheerful and optimistic. Emotionally you are happy-go-lucky and hedonistic. You are self-sufficient and self-reliant, and deeply emotionally involved in all undertakings. You love display and pageants, especially if you are personally involved in them. This may lead you to being involved in drama, whether on the stage or in the home. You feel that you can do anything that you want and your creative ability feels as though it has no bounds. You may appear to others to be haughty and somewhat spoilt. This is because you have a tendency to think of yourself as royalty and the rest of humanity as your subjects. You have a need to be admired and even applauded and you are constantly seeking appreciation and attention. You have a natural creative flair in the home with a gift for interior design and your

The 12 Moon Signs

surroundings will always be flamboyant and probably expensive. You think of your home as your palace and, in seeking to impress others, you may well overspend at times. You are a social climber and demand respect from all those around you. You are straightforward and usually dignified, enabling you to gain responsibility and status. Nothing hurts you more than when you feel unappreciated and your pride has been stepped upon. You have a natural nobility, but you can be egocentric and even pompous. It is very difficult for you to back down or accept any sort of compromise – after all you are the Ruler.

You are a loving and devoted parent and will cosset and play with your children with great affection and warmth. You love giving and have a great sense of charity towards those worse off than you. You are highly emotional with a strong drive for power and prominence.

Above: you are a loving and devoted parent and will cosset and play with your children with great affection and warmth.

The 12 Moon Signs

VIRGO

Virgo Moons are reserved, analytical and critical. You may seem unemotional to others as it is difficult for you to express what you feel. Consequently, you can come across as cold and detached and sometimes even prudish and stuffy, when in fact you are highly emotional and easily hurt.

You may have a deep-seated inferiority complex which may lead you to proving yourself through your intellectual superiority. You always consider the practical application of study rather than just learning for its own sake.

You are generally shy and so respond well to encouragement and appreciation, although you rarely give this to others. You are your own worst enemy and assume that because you are over-critical of yourself that others are the same. You have very little in the way of self-esteem. You may feel that people don't like you, for this

The 12 Moon Signs

is a placement that shows much lack of self-esteem, thus you tend to be emotionally reserved. Your talents lie in expressing your feelings through writing and poetry as your Moon is ruled by Mercury, the messenger god. Consequently you will be ruled by your mind rather than by your heart and you will have trouble understanding highly emotional and passionate people. Your reactions often seem detached and rather cold. Self-analysis may occupy a lot of your thoughts and in fact psychoanalysis and psychiatry would be good careers for you.

You are too introverted to have a strong sex drive and you will be shy about the physical act and have

difficulty in accepting its undignified side. Within a relationship you will attempt to make yourself indispensable to your partner, thereby securing your love, and you respond well to responsibility. In the home you are particularly concerned with hygiene, health and diet and will be constantly involved in tidying up and cleaning.

Virgo Moon is an earthy moon so you are practical and have a definite sense of the realities of life. You are at your best when you are taking care of someone who is in need of you. You can be temperamental and argumentative, but you have a shrewd business sense and pay meticulous attention to detail.

The 12 Moon Signs

LIBRA

Libra Moons are gentle and tolerant, and have a great sense of beauty and justice. You are, above all things, dependent upon your personal relationships. The symbol of Libra, the scales, signifies balance and symmetry in all things. You are diplomatic, broad-minded, social and make pleasant company. You dislike disorder and spend a great deal of your time organising your busy social life. You are even-tempered, well-mannered and graceful in movement. As you are ruled by Venus, art and beauty are paramount in your life, as is your search for the perfect partner. You cannot bear coarseness or vulgarity and will seek relationships with cultured and educated people.

You are highly adaptable and dislike disputes, conflicts and disorder. Your gentle nature will bring you many friends, although, because of your tendency to weigh things in the balance, you may never be sure of how you feel about people. You can find it hard to make up your mind quickly and will spend a great deal of time considering the various possibilities and options open to you in all areas of your life.

The 12 Moon Signs

Your home, which is very important to you, will be harmonious and tranquil and full of beautiful objects. You are particularly attracted towards the arts and may make a career in this direction. Anything that you can make more beautiful will be given a makeover, including people.

You enjoy the company of people and do not like to spend much time alone. You need to be liked and your emotional well-being depends on being appreciated for the beautiful person that you really are, for you truly are a thoughtful and good-natured person who will go out of their way to be kind to others. At many times in your life you will seem to be in crisis and have difficulty in making decisions because you are capable of seeing both sides equally. As often as not your decision will be based on the toss of a coin. You can sometimes be too willing to compromise and frequently allow others to take advantage of you in the name of peace and because it is easier to let other people make decisions. For your partner you can be self-sacrificing and happy to fulfil his or her needs before your own.

A solid, steady relationship is your preference. You love to receive small gifts and you are a romantic at heart. You do your best to spread beauty and harmony wherever you can.

SCORPIO

Scorpio Moons are the most passionate and secretive of all the signs. You are highly sensitive and have an uncanny memory which leads you to remember both pleasant and unpleasant memories which can sometimes leave deep psychic scars. You enjoy life to the full and have an innate understanding that through suffering character is formed. You are the most sexual of all signs, but you combine your sexuality with deep spirituality.

Pluto, the ruler of the underworld, can lead you into the depths of your unconscious where you may find disturbing feelings but, having entered into your underworld, you return strangely refreshed and born anew. You have a great capacity for regeneration and will die many times in your lifetime. Change is what you thrive on. You need to learn to come to terms with your deep emotions as other signs are not as emotionally intense as you. You may find that

The 12 Moon Signs

you see other people as shallow. Your real nature is not apparent to others as, until you get to know somebody deeply, you tend to hide your true feelings. But once you love, you love passionately and the object of your affection can take over your whole existence. This can also be so for your children as you will bestow an all-consuming love upon them. You are a good homemaker, provided that you get your own way in it, but you prefer the company of your immediate family rather than entertaining all and sundry.

In all your relationships you are extremely possessive and jealous and can even become violent when your passions are thwarted. No-one says "no" to a Scorpio Moon. You can be domineering and will often use your sexual favours to get what you want. You have a problem with judging people too quickly and, if they make a mistake, you rarely give them a second chance. You react to emotional situations in an abrupt and impulsive way. You can also be vindictive, spiteful and vengeful when wronged and are easily hurt. You are very determined in achieving your ambitions and thrive on new challenges. You are an extremist by nature and never pursue anything light-heartedly; even when a situation becomes detrimental you insist on seeing it through to the end.

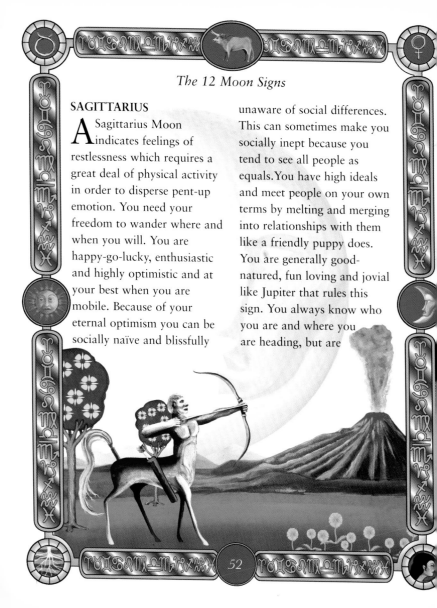

The 12 Moon Signs

SAGITTARIUS

A Sagittarius Moon indicates feelings of restlessness which requires a great deal of physical activity in order to disperse pent-up emotion. You need your freedom to wander where and when you will. You are happy-go-lucky, enthusiastic and highly optimistic and at your best when you are mobile. Because of your eternal optimism you can be socially naïve and blissfully unaware of social differences. This can sometimes make you socially inept because you tend to see all people as equals. You have high ideals and meet people on your own terms by melting and merging into relationships with them like a friendly puppy does. You are generally good-natured, fun loving and jovial like Jupiter that rules this sign. You always know who you are and where you are heading, but are

adaptable enough to change direction when it feels that you will learn more.

Learning is very important to you, although you have a tendency not to learn from your mistakes. The learning that you are interested in is the knowledge of all things, particularly the mysteries of the universe. You make a fine teacher or spiritual adviser.

Your home may not be tidy but it is filled with objects that you have gathered on your travels. You are very enthusiastic in teaching your children everything they want to know and encouraging them to expand their knowledge whenever you can, being more of a friend than a parent.

It is important to you that your partners are also your friends as well as your lovers. You display your affections openly and need a partner who will play, socialise and travel places with you without making too many demands. Being free and without restraints is one of your deepest needs.

Sporting activities will help keep your weight down as you have a predisposition to over-indulge in eating and drinking.

You are prone to many changes in your life, particularly to changes of residence or career which you need to fulfil your restless nature.

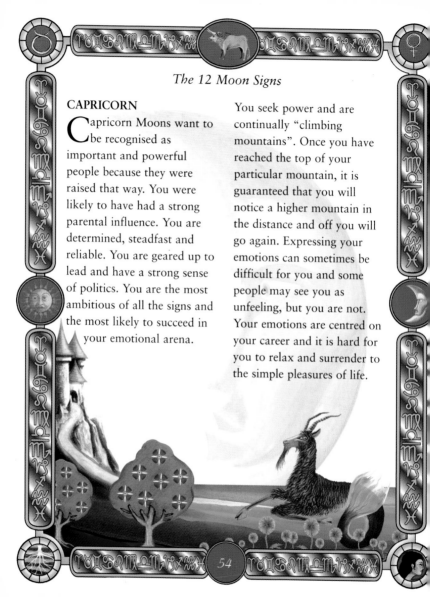

CAPRICORN

Capricorn Moons want to be recognised as important and powerful people because they were raised that way. You were likely to have had a strong parental influence. You are determined, steadfast and reliable. You are geared up to lead and have a strong sense of politics. You are the most ambitious of all the signs and the most likely to succeed in your emotional arena.

You seek power and are continually "climbing mountains". Once you have reached the top of your particular mountain, it is guaranteed that you will notice a higher mountain in the distance and off you will go again. Expressing your emotions can sometimes be difficult for you and some people may see you as unfeeling, but you are not. Your emotions are centred on your career and it is hard for you to relax and surrender to the simple pleasures of life.

The 12 Moon Signs

You are the parent of the Zodiac because you are ruled by Saturn, the god of time. Because of this, you are likely to seem old when you are young and young when you are old. Some Moon in Capricorns have a Peter Pan complex but only inside; on the outside they appear to be wise beyond their years. Whatever your goals are you will strive to achieve them, stubbornly and persistently. You are a very hard worker and will take on goals that would frighten other signs.

You are conservative in your emotions, not in a political sense, but in a true sense of conservation. This is your way – not to create new things but to improve upon and conserve what has come before you. If you are thwarted in your goals, you can become despondent and moody and begin to look at the negative side of things. You need to develop a more optimistic approach to life. Capricorn Moons can be shy but have a very clever sense of humour and can lead people to do what they want with this humour.

Your home life, like your career, will be ambitious. You will want to live in the best house in the best part of town. A Capricorn Moon loves renovating old property and your taste is normally classical. A lot of Capricorn Moons work from home due to their tendency to be shy

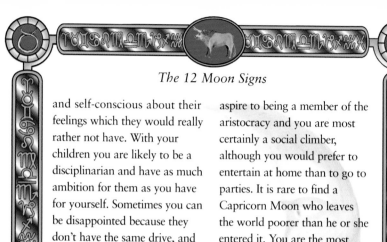

and self-conscious about their feelings which they would really rather not have. With your children you are likely to be a disciplinarian and have as much ambition for them as you have for yourself. Sometimes you can be disappointed because they don't have the same drive, and it can be hard for you to show your deep feelings of affection towards them. You may aspire to being a member of the aristocracy and you are most certainly a social climber, although you would prefer to entertain at home than to go to parties. It is rare to find a Capricorn Moon who leaves the world poorer than he or she entered it. You are the most reserved of signs, particularly in the way you communicate and interact with others. Your driving ambitions are usually successful but sometimes at the cost of romantic life.

Security and stability are very important to you as are financial gain and establishing yourself as a community leader. You are a traditionalist in life and have solid values and morals.

The 12 Moon Signs

AQUARIUS

Aquarius Moons produce the most modern and progressive people of all the signs. However, you can sometimes be erratic in some of the ideals you hold. You are unusual and unpredictable, with a broad imagination. You are most likely to engage in many kinds of group activities and have a wide range of friends from all walks of life. You have a capacity to see inside people and not be taken in by appearances. For you a beggar may be an angel in disguise.

You have a very creative imagination and your many friends will value your input into their lives. Sometimes your high ideals can get in the way of practicality and common sense. You have a quality that puts you ahead of your time and some people may see you as downright eccentric. You are attracted to all things that are modern and innovative as you are ruled by Uranus, the god of change. You love the sciences and would dearly love to invent something to improve the lot of humanity.

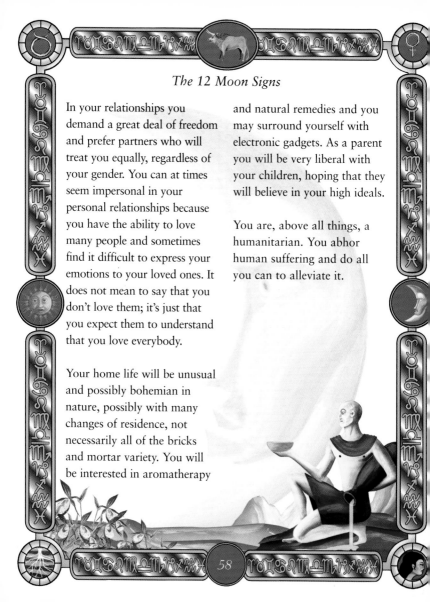

The 12 Moon Signs

In your relationships you demand a great deal of freedom and prefer partners who will treat you equally, regardless of your gender. You can at times seem impersonal in your personal relationships because you have the ability to love many people and sometimes find it difficult to express your emotions to your loved ones. It does not mean to say that you don't love them; it's just that you expect them to understand that you love everybody.

Your home life will be unusual and possibly bohemian in nature, possibly with many changes of residence, not necessarily all of the bricks and mortar variety. You will be interested in aromatherapy and natural remedies and you may surround yourself with electronic gadgets. As a parent you will be very liberal with your children, hoping that they will believe in your high ideals.

You are, above all things, a humanitarian. You abhor human suffering and do all you can to alleviate it.

PISCES

A Moon in Pisces means that you have a great understanding of what it is to be human, albeit in a somewhat dreamy sense. You are gifted with great sensitivity and perception, allowing you to have great compassion and consideration for other people. This Moon means you have great empathy towards others in a psychic way and you often experience their emotions.

Since Neptune, the god of the sea, rules your Moon, you need to ensure that you are not flooded by people's moods and desires psychically. Therefore you should meditate and reflect on your own feelings in solitude.

Life to you is permanently rose-tinted, no matter how harsh the reality. Everyone's "little faults" are ignored, no matter how big.

At times, though, your over-optimism and unselfishness can leave you open to others taking advantage of your passive nature. Your misplaced trust means that you often end up hurt and feeling sorry for yourself. Rather than blame the other person, you tend to turn in on

yourself, again resulting in melancholy.

You will spend a great deal of your time searching for answers to life's great questions and will read a great many books on a wide variety of subjects. At times you will seek a more spiritual way of life. You are surprisingly ambitious and, because of your gift of creative visualisation, you can achieve your goals.

However, you do not have the competitive drive of other signs and so can lack self-confidence.

Trust is something that you do not give freely. When you are entirely comfortable with someone you can then be surprisingly bossy as this is your way of showing that you trust them. In marriage you are so supportive that you are in danger of becoming a martyr. You need love and approval and, although you are happy to live alone, you prefer to give and receive love.

Sometimes you can be so shy and repressed that you do not find the love you require and

The 12 Moon Signs

instead retreat into yourself. As a parent you empathise with your children but prefer those that can actively respond rather than young babies.

You are incredibly romantic and love all the little things which make up a relationship. Sex is something you enjoy as it combines all your favourite feelings and sensations.

Your home is your haven, a place where you can withdraw from the hustle and bustle of everyday life. However, you will also have many friends and visitors coming and going, particularly as you rarely lock your doors. People are drawn to you because they know that you are a good shoulder

to cry on and will assist as much as possible with their personal problems. You need to ensure, however, that you do not sacrifice yourself for others too much.

Above: as a parent you empathise with your children but prefer those that can actively respond rather than young babies.

TAURUS SUN
AND THE 12 MOON SIGN COMBINATIONS

When you calculate a birth chart you will discover that the Moon as well as the planets will sometimes be in different signs of the Zodiac. The whole chart gives the whole picture of the personality, but the Sun and the Moon have the most powerful effect upon us. When you combine the Sun sign and the Moon sign you are combining different parts of the Zodiac. Some signs work well together and some signs don't, in the same way that two Sun signs may live in eternal conflict where others live in harmony; so it is with the Sun and Moon in your chart. What follows is an explanation of the combinations between your Sun and various other moons that may appear in your birth chart.

TAURUS SUN WITH ARIES MOON

The combination of your earthy Sun sign with the fiery Moon in Aries makes you a determined individualist with a very strong drive towards your goals. The peaceful and placid attributes of Taurus combined with the assertiveness of Aries can make you very dogmatic but give you a sparkling enthusiasm and stimulate your leadership traits. You have a searching mind and when you find inconsistencies in logic the quickness of Aries comes into play enabling you to form opinions on any matter rapidly. However, there are conflicting sides to your nature, much more than you may realise or even admit. You can be tolerant in your viewpoint one minute and totally unreasonable the next. You seem to have a way of making your wishes known by a manner or a gesture. When you are arguing a point you have a way of being so plausible and reasonable that you quickly wear down any resistance. You are assertive and have a way of eliminating opposition by the force of your willpower.

If you harness these traits and control them, there is little that you cannot accomplish. You find it difficult to interact with people, so you will achieve most in work which does not involve much in the way of personal contact. Engineering, for example, or any work within the building industry would suit you well.

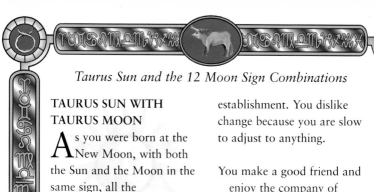

Taurus Sun and the 12 Moon Sign Combinations

TAURUS SUN WITH TAURUS MOON

As you were born at the New Moon, with both the Sun and the Moon in the same sign, all the traits of Taurus will be amplified, particularly the determination and purposeful nature of Taurus. Your concentration and staying power is strong. When you apply your mind to something, nothing can distract you. You can focus with great tenacity equally on work or play. You are not one to jump to conclusions easily but when you do you rarely modify your views. You are highly conventional and have a great regard for the establishment. You dislike change because you are slow to adjust to anything.

You make a good friend and enjoy the company of congenial people, particularly artistic ones. You love good food, good music and the good life in general. You are very loyal and faithful to your lovers and will lavish affection on them.

This is one of the most materialistic of combinations and you have a special knack for investments. You work hard and do not mind beginning at the bottom and slowly and determinedly working your way up to the top. You will achieve success

because the work you do is done well and you are trustworthy and reliable. You are serene and patient and you will use your humour to charm your opponents until you get your own way. You respect authority figures because some day you expect to become one. Whatever you do in the world will endure beyond your time.

TAURUS SUN WITH GEMINI MOON

When the Sun in Taurus is combined with a Gemini Moon a highly sociable person with a very straightforward and pleasant personality is indicated. However, the contrasting elements of the slowness of Taurus and the speed of Gemini can make you more prone to errors of judgement. The Bull's stubbornness is ever present but the Moon's influence may cause you to jump to conclusions based on superficial information. Problems may become apparent if you form an opinion without knowing all the facts as then nothing will sway you from it, even if you are incorrect.

Above: you are serene and patient and you will use your humour to charm your opponents until you get your own way.

Taurus Sun and the 12 Moon Sign Combinations

You are mentally restless but lack the memory indicated by Taurus. You tend to be over-critical of others. This is the most fickle of the Taurus combinations. You may find yourself constantly falling in love and then finding out the other person is not the "right one". You have a short attention span so you need continual challenges and stimulation to keep you interested. It is important for you to stimulate your mind as much as possible through education in order to stabilise your fickle nature and increase your capacity for success. In particular, your talents in oral and written communication will be a great advantage in your career so work in the media or public relations would be ideal. Unusually for a Taurus you would find marketing a good choice.

Above: you have a short attention span so you need continual challenges and stimulation to keep you interested.

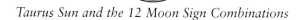

Taurus Sun and the 12 Moon Sign Combinations

TAURUS SUN WITH CANCER MOON

This combination of Sun and Moon signs blends the watery sensitivity of Cancer with the stubbornness and will of Taurus. This can create great conflict in your nature as at times you are given to pushing people around and enforcing your will but without the emotional belligerence of Taurus. You are over-diplomatic at times in your efforts to avoid conflict and this means that you are easily hurt and occasionally bitter towards others. In business you are a good tactician, using your feelings to develop strategies rather than logic but, because you are so sensitive, your emotions are easily aroused. The most stabilising factors in your life are your home and family and you should look to them if you are upset.

On the surface you may seem self-assured, but this can be a front to hide your low self-esteem. You have a talent for counselling but sometimes it seems that you have no real convictions of your own. You tend to keep quiet about your own achievements and your own knowledge, particularly when difficult decisions are involved. However, your ideas are usually sound and well-constructed, your ambitions are strong and you rarely give up on a job. You do have a

tendency to be somewhat negative and pessimistic when life does not go the way you want it to. You should, therefore, learn to have more confidence in yourself and to stand up for your beliefs.

You are particularly well suited to a career in the catering and hospitality industry.

TAURUS SUN WITH LEO MOON

This Sun and fiery Moon sign combination is one of the strongest in terms of willpower – think raging bull with fierce lion. Nothing stands in your way when you make up your mind. You are frank, honest and fearless and your opinions are well thought out. Although you respect other people's opinions, you trust yourself

Above: you are particularly well suited to a career in the catering and hospitality industry.

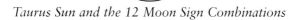

Taurus Sun and the 12 Moon Sign Combinations

and your personal abilities first and foremost. You do not rely on your intellect alone but depend on your instincts, too. You have high self-esteem which leads to success in all your undertakings. You are excellent at organising and planning, making you superb management material as people enjoy working with you. When you take on a project you see it through from start to finish. Sometimes your personal pride can make you seem domineering and bossy. This is because you possess strong likes and dislikes and you are not afraid to show them.

You rarely lose your temper but can be critical although you are always fair. You hate to be scrutinised because you want things done your way. You are trustworthy and devoted to your close friends but tend to make snap judgements about people, following your instincts, rather than your reason. You have a very stable personality but with a tendency towards extremes on occasion. Behind the impulsive and proud front of your personality lies a practical, reliable and determined nature that serves you well.

A career in the entertainment industry, either in the spotlight or behind the scenes, would work well for you. You could particularly develop your talents in singing and dancing.

TAURUS WITH VIRGO MOON

This combination of both an earthy Sun sign and an earthy Moon sign produces a very common-sense approach to life. Your charm and poise will help you glide through life with very few obstacles. This is because the stable, physical characteristics of Taurus are blended with Virgo's calm intelligence. However, although you have much to offer, you need a great deal of encouragement to get you going. Once this inertia is overcome you then throw yourself into work with great vigour. You need the stimulation of life's little problems to keep you going and, whilst they may cause you to complain, they are vital in terms of ensuring you work to your maximum potential. When you do apply yourself to something, the results are amazing.

Your mind is quick and retentive so you make a natural academic. You read many books and remember things that others may overlook. You do not like taking orders but, because you are not very aggressive or assertive, you are inclined to end up in a subordinate role. This may cause you some

Taurus Sun and the 12 Moon Sign Combinations

resentment at times but is for the best as you do not like responsibility. It also allows you to concentrate on the fine details. You are charismatic and have a capacity to see people for what they really are. All these characteristics combined should give you an easy life and a comfortable lifestyle. You are particularly suited to a career in nutrition, hygiene and the medical profession in general.

TAURUS SUN WITH LIBRA MOON

In this combination both your Sun sign and Moon sign are ruled by the planet Venus which bestows on you one of the most charming and likeable personalities amongst all the combinations. A beautiful home and a loving family, along with good friends, are your first loves and you do all that you can to ensure that you keep them. You have an easygoing outlook on life, backed up with a fine sense of humour which gives you a keen social persona. You are always optimistic, even when you are weighed down with your private problems. If anyone does dislike you they are more than likely motivated by jealousy.

You have strong inclinations towards the arts, particularly drama. Your positive attitude allows you to accomplish great things when you put your mind to it, but your sensual nature can give you a tendency to laziness. You find conflict unpleasant and vulgar and confrontational situations or hostility can make you ill. Normally your Libran sense of balance and ability to weigh things up keeps you from losing your temper. Your wide range of emotional responses can take you from ecstatic heights when you are in love to the depths of despair when confronted by hostile energies.

TAURUS SUN WITH SCORPIO MOON

You were born around the time of the Full Moon and the combination of a fixed Sun sign and a fixed Moon sign indicates deep emotional intensity which is unusual in the normally stable Taurus Sun sign. You have 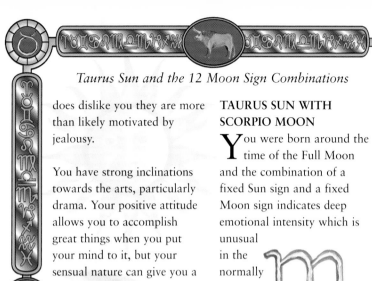 a secretive nature and so often hide your deepest emotions, allowing them to fester. As the signs are polar opposites there is a fanatical side to you. You do not see the subtleties in life; black is black and white is white and for you the many shades of grey do not exist.

You are highly passionate, strong-willed and know what you want and how to get it.

To the opposite sex you are charming and have an animal magnetism. However, close personal relationships can break down quickly because of your nasty temper. You excel at drama and need to be the centre of attention at all times. No one could call you timid. With your fierce independence you are likely to go far in any work that you choose. Forensics and crime investigation are ideal career paths for you.

It is not that you are highly ambitious but you just seem to have a flair for success. Within you there is a tension that constantly builds up and needs releasing. You often feel that you want to escape from it all and you can become very stressed if you feel trapped. It is very likely that at every Full Moon you will experience emotional release from the tensions of life.

Above: you have a secretive nature and so often hide your deepest emotions, allowing them to fester.

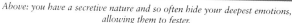

Taurus Sun and the 12 Moon Sign Combinations

TAURUS SUN WITH SAGITTARIUS MOON

The combination of an earthy but fixed Sun sign with a fiery and mutable Moon sign transforms the simple earthy and stable nature of the Bull into a much more adventurous and outgoing person. You are an extrovert with a highly developed social sense. You love people but they must be "your kind of people". You do not enjoy dull or uninteresting people and would rather be alone than tolerate them. You can be selective but you do have the skills necessary to get along with all types of people if you need to. You communicate in a very direct and blunt way and have no difficulty in being understood. You have a decisive mind but can express yourself in a flexible way which enables you to discuss a pet subject at great length. You do have a tendency to hold to very high principles and moral codes and you are not above sitting in judgement on others. In fact, you are well-suited to the legal and publishing professions. You are conventional and law-abiding and more than likely part of the establishment. You can apply yourself to studying any subject with great determination and love gossip and rumour. You are likely to have a full and satisfying intellectual life and a pleasant and luxurious home life.

TAURUS SUN WITH CAPRICORN MOON

The double earth combination of your Sun and Moon gives a strong and durable emotional makeup, with the ability to handle stresses and strains and to emerge unscathed from any crisis For you every cloud has a silver lining and you have the ability to turn any obstacle to your advantage. You are normally easygoing unless someone provokes you or you are asked to do something against your beliefs. Then you resist with all your might. You are stable and decisive and rarely frivolous. You are too practical for daydreaming and spend most of your time engaged in practical affairs. You have a talent for critical analysis and you are respected enough that others will ask your opinion.

Because of your strong sense of responsibility and need for the recognition and power that usually accompanies authority, politics is a very attractive career path to you. Although you will probably achieve it, you are not really looking for wealth. Position and prestige are far more important to you. You have a strong sense of your own worth which you like to see manifest either in your accomplishments or in your surroundings. You have a

keen understanding of human nature and an uncanny instinct for knowing what people are thinking. You are also good at solving problems in a very down-to-earth way. Domestic stability is of the utmost importance to you and one of your main aspirations will be for a magnificent house for you and your family to live in.

TAURUS SUN WITH AQUARIUS MOON

The double fixed qualities of your Sun and Moon signs give solid convictions that, once formed, will be difficult to change, no matter how good the argument against them is. You do, however, have an extremely friendly and easygoing personality and you know instinctively how to get along with people, including strangers. This magnetic Sun and Moon combination draws many people to you who can help you achieve your aims in life. You are tolerant towards other people's views and always very interested in them, whilst remaining detached. You do possess a

Above: domestic stability is important to you and one of your main aspirations will be for a magnificent house for you and your family to live in.

good deal of self-esteem that will help you to attain your goals, which mainly centre on improving the world. Your friendliness is your greatest asset, but you will discover that few people can live up to your idealistic expectations of how the world should be.

As your emotions are well under control you rarely lose your temper. Your major motivation stems from your deep feelings yet, because of the impersonal aspect of Aquarius, you are rarely likely to show them. You are good at controlling and directing your emotions to facilitate your innovative ideas. You have a very curious, inventive and studious mind and are not particularly materialistic. A career in IT or electronics would suit you well. As a business person you have shrewd judgement but always retain a code of honour. You also have the ability to work with colour, especially in the field of interior design. You are particularly attracted to modern art forms.

Above: a career in IT or electronics would suit you well.

Taurus Sun and the 12 Moon Sign Combinations

TAURUS SUN WITH PISCES MOON

The fixed and earthy Taurus Sun combined with the watery and mutable Pisces Moon feeds your imagination and creates for you a private dream world so that sometimes you seem to lose your grip on reality. You do take life seriously but see things happening around you as though you were watching a movie. Your Taurean nature gives you an inner stability but the influence of your Moon gives you a need to isolate yourself. You require constant sympathy and affection because you are supersensitive on an emotional level. You are impressionable in romance and must be careful not to be imposed upon by lovers or friends. It is important that you select your friends carefully as they can easily influence you to over-indulge in food, sex and pleasure-seeking. You are extremely amiable and respond to people in a spontaneous and natural manner. You do have a stubborn streak, however, which for you is a helpful and protective device. You should avoid brooding and feeling sorry for yourself. You have a highly creative imagination and, if you work at it, you can turn many of your dreams into reality. You

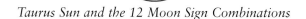

Taurus Sun and the 12 Moon Sign Combinations

could at sometime in your life be drawn to religion or the mystical side of life, If you find that things get too much for you then you must find somewhere to spend some time alone to recharge your batteries.

Above: you require constant sympathy and affection because you are supersensitive on an emotional level.

EPILOGUE

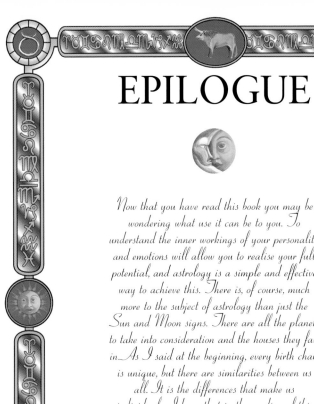

*Now that you have read this book you may be
wondering what use it can be to you. To
understand the inner workings of your personality
and emotions will allow you to realise your full
potential, and astrology is a simple and effective
way to achieve this. There is, of course, much
more to the subject of astrology than just the
Sun and Moon signs. There are all the planets
to take into consideration and the houses they fall
in. As I said at the beginning, every birth chart
is unique, but there are similarities between us
all. It is the differences that make us
individuals. I hope that in the reading of this
book perhaps you will be inspired to look deeper
into yourself and deeper into the uses of
astrology.*

"Know yourself and the truth will set you free"